For Corporate Clients

Increase Sales 25% Guaranteed

Principe's Principles Specifically for

DEVELOPERS, BUILDERS & REALTORS

Lou Principe

Dedication Page

Sometimes someone comes along in your life and says one thing to you that hits home and changes your life completely. This book is dedicated to that person, my real estate mentor Colonel Joe Baum, who with his wife Ida, owned Baum Reality. I rented an apartment from them in 1968. When I first met Joe, I thought he was a crazy old man. A short time later, he became my real estate hero. When I was working as a police officer in Hollywood, Florida in 1969, Joe told me I might get killed being a cop and that I should get my real estate license. Joe had purchased all of Hollywood Beach, Florida in 1922 for $100 an acre. He was the shrewdest businessman I ever met.

I would also like to dedicate this book to my dad Frank Principe. He became my role model for work ethic by working three shifts a day as a waiter at the Waldorf-Astoria and Savoy Hilton.

The very first training seminar I ever attended was presented by Jack Gazzardo. It was based on Xerox Sales Training Systems, which most industries subsequently adopted. This book is also dedicated to him.

Finally, I'd like to thank all the negative people I've come across in my life who have inspired me with the following advice: "You're crazy; get a real job making an hourly wage; it can't be done; you can't fight the system; if it were any good, someone else would be doing it; it's not the right timing; it's not the right season; it's not possible; it's too easy; you don't have the proper credentials; you don't have the education; you don't have the money," and so on. Without them to motivate me, I never would have achieved the success I have.

I owe this book to God. My life is an example of how God inspired men and women to come to the United States to pursue their dreams. You can accomplish anything in the United States provided you are willing to make a commitment to it!

Legal Stuff

THE ART OF PRE-SELLING HOMES

Lou Principe

ISBN-13: 978-0-9850269-6-7
1. Real Estate 2. Self Help 3. New Age 4. Sales
First Edition Library of Congress # pending

INTRODUCTION

Most developers, homebuilders, and real estate agents think circumstances control their sales. In the next few pages, you'll learn to see a different dimension to the home building and real estate industries.

Sound impossible? Unbelievable? Incredible? This book will give you an easy step-by-step scientific formula for how to take control of your sales. Some of us think we are doing everything possible, but a wise person always looks at all the options available.

This is not a classroom book based on a theory, though you will learn some theory along the way. More accurately, what you are about to read is a theorem, an exact scientific formula that if used properly will consistently bring about immediate sales. The Principe Program has been used by the largest homebuilders in the nation with immediate measurable and sustainable results.

On my website you'll find documentary evidence of sales increasing from 100% to 1,000%, the latter being verified by the University of South Florida. There are numerous reference letters, video clips and articles from major builders, Fortune 100 companies, universities, and government agencies, all documenting unrefuted evidence of the near instantaneous results achieved.

One of the most important questions I ask my clients is, "Do you know what your sales department is doing with your inventory?" I'm not talking about lot, house, or listing inventory. I'm asking about *people* inventory – the customer. It's a CEO's fatal error to ignore this important question. Some CEOs spend less that two percent of their time in an area that brings in 100% of the income. Are you a CEO—Creator of Enormous

Opportunities or a CEO—Creator of Enormous Obstacles?

Individual sales consultants would do well to conduct a careful study of conversion factors, i.e., the number of customers coming in versus actual sales. Conversion rates are the only measurable unit in this industry sufficiently reliable for tracking what the sales department is doing with your advertising and marketing dollars. But we now have another tool, a way to establish a baseline for the salesperson to measure their progress.

If you were to increase your closing ratios from 3% to 4%, that would mean a 25% increase in your sales. A mere 1% increase to a national builder represents millions of dollars in additional profits without one cent of additional advertising cost. Most builders don't measure conversion factors as specifically as they should, and if they do, they do not realize the importance.
The reporting process must be reviewed daily and weekly. This becomes our smoke detector in the field; it will warn us before a blaze gets out of hand.

Every time a guest walks through the door, they are treated by most salespeople as a traffic unit, or "up" (an industry term indicating it's your time to get up off your chair) and not as a real person.

By the time a real person who spends an average of forty-five minutes driving to your property walks into your model home, you have already spent an average of $500.00 in advertising and model upkeep costs to bring them there. Every time a guest walks out without buying your home, it costs you hundreds of thousands of dollars in lost profits.

The instinct is to work the obviously hot prospects and to allow the rest of the tire-kickers to move on to some other development.

The number of sales that are lost as a result of this crude approach is hard to evaluate, but over the years, your experience and mine teaches us the loss is enormous.

Now that we have established a baseline, let us discuss the blueprint or plan. Managers and salespeople must be made aware that every person who comes into the model is a potential purchaser or knows someone who may be.

People say they are just looking because they don't want to get involved with a salesperson and risk being sold. People are generally afraid of salespeople.

Think of the last time you went into a department store. Did a sales clerk walk up to you and say, "Can I help you?" You probably responded, "No, I'm just looking." What triggered that response? It was probably the manner in which the sales clerk approached you. Did you actually drive to the department store without any latent motivation to purchase? Of course not.

We need to change our perception of our customers. I refer to a person looking at a model home as a "guest" who should be welcomed and treated as you would welcome and treat a new guest in your own home.

In various surveys done with my clients and their *guests* (not traffic units) we found 25% of the "just lookers" purchase within thirty days if they didn't have a house to sell. The only problem is that the guest purchased from your competition.

We need to understand that the client comes out to your property to purchase; that is a fact. The average client travels forty-five minutes one way and forty-five minutes back home, only to spend less than five minutes face to face with a salesperson in transactional time.

We need to fully appreciate that the client has come to us to explore the possibility of purchasing our home, but that is all we know about them until we can identify their personality type. Reading their verbal and nonverbal cues will help us determine how best to help them.

Did you feel any fear or apprehension from them as they walked in the door? How could you tell? What were the cues? A nervous person may perspire or have a wet handshake. Their breathing may be rapid and shallow. This tells you they are nervous, so you can employ various techniques to help them relax.

It is essential to read the nonverbal cues as soon as they walk in the door. Reading nonverbal cues comprises 55% of our communication ability and tells us whether they are serious buyers.

Aside from their verbal and nonverbal communication, there are many visual cues as to their personality type. For instance, if they drive a later model vehicle and wear a gray or navy suit with a white shirt, they are likely to be a "director" personality type. This type of person likes to feel in control. Therefore, let them be in control. If they want a brochure, give them one. If they want a price, give it to them. Once they have what they want, they are more likely to relax and then you can begin to interact with them.

Other personality types are "the relater" who relaxes by finding something in common with you; "the socializer" who is the life of the party (so be sure to have a few good jokes for them); and "the thinker" who needs validation in order to buy; he or she wants to know how other smart people have purchased so they feel safe and secure in their decision.

You have to become a chameleon and adjust your personality style to theirs in order to make the sale. You will find some of your customers have similar personality styles to you or your friends. Those customers will be easier to relate to. Others may have different styles that may pose more of a challenge. For those, you need to match their style.

The only thing standing between the salesperson and the client purchasing is the communication ability of the salesperson. If your soft skills are lacking, you may not notice the client's nonverbal communications and metamessages (underlying messages) but they are equally as important—if not more important—than what the client is verbalizing.

Seminar taught body language as selling tool

By: Barry Pollock
Bonded Builders Home
Warranty Association

When I first walked into the Sales & Marketing Council's educational presentation on Oct 30 featuring Lou Principe, sales trainer, the thought was going through my mind was "who is this guy?"

Three hours later, when I left the seminar, two thoughts were going through my mind: where has this guy been all my life and where were all of the Associate members?

Did you lose out on this fantastic learning experience presented by your Association?

The name of this seminar was "The Psychology of Selling." It deliberately had no reference to new home sales in the promotional literature because it was intended to be a seminar about selling anything.

The last time I looked Associate members were part of the Association so they could network with and hopefully sell their products and services to the builder members.

Surprise! That is just what Principe was prepared to teach had you decided to make a small investment in your own future.

Since you decided not to attend, the room was filled with on-site sale people (and builders, too) and Principe tailored his presentation to the needs of his audience.

An audience, by the way, which stayed glued to their chairs until 9:22 p.m. (usually the exodus starts shortly after 8:30), which is a tribute to how effective Principe's presentation was...even to seasoned professionals.

Principle taught how to read the pupils of the prospect's eyes to determine when we have hit their hot buttons.

He taught how to read the direction of the prospect's feet to verify if they were paying attention.

He showed how to get a prospect to willingly sit down an talk to us.

If you think that learning skills such as these will only help on site sales people do more business...then you were right to stay away.

If you can see and can figure out how learning skills such as these might just add to your bottom line, then I strongly suggest you make it a point to attend the next sales and marketing seminar.

It will be in F...

It is imperative that we initiate effective communication through establishing a common bond with our new found friend, the client. People buy people, not necessarily the product.

It's our responsibility to break the barrier of being strangers and communicate effectively enough to become friends.

How well is your team getting to know facts about their new friends? Wouldn't you agree with me that we need to find out what is in the client's mind about housing? They're not going to divulge their innermost personal thoughts to a stranger.

People Buy People

What are we doing in the sales office to make the client comfortable? We have the home court advantage because we are secure in our environment.

What are the clients feeling as they drive into your parking lot? What conversations go on in the car before they walk into the model? Are they overwhelmed with fear and apprehension of being in unfamiliar territory, compounded by the fact that you are the expert, a professional salesperson asking:

> "Can I help you?
> "Are you interested in a home today?"
> "Fill out this registration card, and I will get you a brochure."

With this standard rote approach, the salesperson hasn't earned the right to ask the client to divulge personal information.

If I were a medical doctor who walked into a room full of patients and said, "Everyone is going to receive a prescription of Tylenol #3," how long do you think I would be in business? We're basically treating everyone who walks into our model homes the same way, regardless of individual sensibilities or motivations.

There must be an individualized selling plan with each purchase. Just as people no longer buy insurance policies, they buy insurance programs designed for their specific needs, neither do they buy houses, but homes suited to their lifestyles.

We are incapable of selling anything to anyone. The best we can hope is to find out everything we need to know about our new friend and assist them in making a purchase decision.

In this industry we need to be housing doctors, listening to the client to determine the best prescription available to suit that particular individual's needs.

Relationship Selling

Clients are both afraid and expectant as they walk through your office door; it's a delicate encounter. Would you agree with me that we need to find out what is in the client's mind about housing? They will not divulge that information to a stranger. We need to communicate effectively to become friends.

People Buy People. It is our responsibility to initiate effective communication through establishing a common bond with a client.

What makes the critical difference between success and failure in selling real estate? It is simply the ability to use those certain soft and social skills with prospective purchasers and the ability to demonstrate how the property matches the client's needs.

Fifty percent of the sale is made within the first two minutes if the client feels comfortable with both you and the environment. The other fifty percent is in subtly calling attention to the features and benefits of the home and the integrity of the builder.

We need to be housing doctors. The patient who just walked into your office has a housing problem. The biggest mistake we make as salespeople is to take out the MLS book or allow the client to go through the models and find their own solutions to the housing problem.

What I often hear – and what you should *never* say is – "Go through the models and I'll be here if you have any questions."

The client is looking for a real estate doctor who can advise them. If I were a doctor and you came into my medical office complaining about a rash under your arm. I would ask, "What type of deodorant do you use?" "What laundry detergent do you use?" "What type of soap do you bathe with?" These would be appropriate questions.

At your prompt, the client will tell you the symptoms if you ask a few important questions regardless of how personal they may be. You are the expert. Your new friend will realize you are the real estate doctor and you are there to help. As the real estate doctor, you have the confidence to take charge of the situation and ask questions. The client expects you to ask questions about their background and housing experiences.

Here are a few funny anecdotes from some of my trainings to illustrate this point:

After conducting a training meeting with U.S. Home in Tampa, Florida, I worked in the model home taking customers as they came in the door, demonstrating these techniques to the new salespeople. A customer walked in and actually said, "I am looking for a housing doctor." The division president looked at me and started laughing. "This is great--she works for you," he joked. "You just talked about being housing doctors in the morning meeting." The client had come in teary-eyed, and because of the division president's remark, she now had a puzzled look on her face. I explained to him that she didn't work for me but was a real client! She had just received a Notice of Divorce and walked into the model home asking to speak with a "housing doctor."

Another time, I came in to a building development as a mystery shopper. During a one-sided presentation, I asked a question. The sales person told me to hold my question, because he had his sales pitch memorized and he would have to start all over again (which he did!).

- The following questions are imperative for a housing doctor to ask:

- Where are your clients from?

- What type of work do they do?

- Where do they work?

- How large is their family?

- What are the names and ages of their children?

- What are their hobbies?

- What house of worship do they attend, if they attend one?

- What room is most important to them and why?

- What do they like about their existing home?

- What do they dislike about their existing home?

- What is the value to the client in purchasing your home?

- If they were to sell their existing home, how much would they list it for?

- What is their equity?

- If it would be possible for the client to change something about their home, what would they change and why?

- Do they like a formal, more traditional, or modern home?

- Are they interested in a great room?

- Do they prefer a split bedroom, or bedrooms all on one side of the house?

- Do they prefer two, three, four, or five bedrooms?

- Do they want one floor or two and why?

- How large a garage and why?

- How long have they lived in their existing home?

- Why are they motivated to move?

- What might prevent them from moving?

- Are they qualified financially, including debt-to-income ratios?

[NOTE: Please make sure your display does not mention a list of "churches." If it does, change it to "houses of worship" because it could be misconstrued that you only cater to certain faiths in your housing development.]

If I were selling new automobile tires, I would ask the client how long they have owned the car, what types of weather they drive in, what types of roads—highway or city streets—and whether they make frequent stops or encounter potholes. All of these are important questions to the client because first, it shows them I am interested in them and that they are important to me. Second, I will decide which tire they need based on their answers.

A professional salesperson needs to be a fact gatherer, a consultant, an analyst. Probe and ask questions in order to find the right house for your client.

We need to stop being information givers and tour guides. Let's get out of our comfort zones and truly transact with the new friend who walked into our home.

Apperception: The Greatest Principle of Selling

Apperception is defined as the process of understanding something perceived in terms of previous experience. The most conclusive certification of human intelligence is the ability to recreate in symbolic form the world in which one lives.

In the truest application of professional salesmanship, we need to recreate the world in which our client lives and openly discuss it. We need to unlock in the client's mind the self-narrated lifestyle as it is right now and create a vision of their future in their new home.

The clients must see clearly that the reward is measurable. We must help them visualize their lives in a particular home.

Effective Model Utilization

The basic psychological principle

I x V = R: Imagination X Vividness = Reality

is one of the most powerful psychological tools you will use to close the sale. You should be able to create in the client's mind a vivid image of them living in their new home.

Once they have made a decision subconsciously, the clients will adapt their behavior patterns to live up to the new self-image you have helped them create.

This vivid personality image of their new home cannot be imitated by a competitor.

Just to say, "This is the bedroom, kitchen, etc." is of no

value to the prospective buyer. Let me assure you, the client knows what room they are in, and they may see a different use for the space.

It's the salesperson's responsibility to take the client through the model effectively.

Remember this: Most homebuyers buy on emotions and justify the purchase with logic after the fact.

They drove to your office or property to look at the possibility of buying a home because they don't like where they are living. Something triggered them to drive to your development, office, or model home.
They are interested in buying a home; otherwise, they could have spent the time and money to do something else. However, they chose not to play golf, go to grandma's, or see a movie; they chose to physically see your property. They are buyers. That's a fact.

Set the Stage

If you're planning to sell the next guest walking through the door, it's imperative that you have the client's sensory responses involved before they enter the home.

The emotions start to flow even before they arrive at your community. They're excited.

From the main road or highway exit, they should see directional signs listing all the amenities you have:

- "Welcome Home!

- "Welcome to Meet & Greet Your Neighbors Tonight

- "Maintenance-Free Homes

- "Clubhouse with Exercise Room" etc.

I refer to these as Silent Sales Signs. As they turn into your community, they should see a nice entry sign, clean streets, late model cars parked in occupied home driveways, freshly painted houses, neat landscaping, and, hopefully, some flowers. (They should see no dog waste, cigarette butts, or litter).

As they are about to exit the car, they turn to each other and possibly discuss your property.

"This looks a lot better than where we are living right now.

"Do you think we can afford it?

"Let's make a promise to each other not to sign anything."

This last statement is called "making a pact," but most break it because I get my new friends involved in the process.

Some people are resentful of salespeople; they are afraid of being sold out. At this point, there is fear and apprehension before they get out of the car. How can you relieve some of that anxiety before they walk in? You do this by getting their sensory receptors involved.

Keep in mind the whole sales process should be a theatrical production, a relatively dramatic moment where the client – and not the salesperson – is the star of the show.

ARE THE PROPS READY?

As they exit the car, do they see and maybe even smell fresh flowers?

You might build a little wooden bridge over the concrete walkway to the model home in order to have the auditory senses involved. The clients hear their own footsteps as they walk over the bridge. You may also consider adding a small bubbling brook or waterfall out front if you don't have one.

I recommend outside speakers with manufactured music, interspersing the builder's or realtor's ads between the songs. The music should be selected based on research of the profiles of potential clients who can afford to buy your home as soon as possible.

We encourage our builders to have a glass entry door so the potential purchaser can see inside to help decrease their anxiety. The salespeople have the home court advantage. They are already accustomed to the office, whereas the client doesn't know what or who is behind the door.

Some salespeople ask, "Can I help you?" "What are you looking for today?" "Fill out my visitor registration card and I'll get a brochure." The metamessage is, "If you don't fill out my card, you don't get a brochure."

We encourage salespeople to treat each customer as a guest as if the salesperson invited them into their own personal home.

Aromas and Food

Smell is an instant recall of childhood memories. When you smell popcorn, what do you think of? Being at home with your parents or going to the movies? What about freshly baked apple pie?

Does the home smell cozy like a home or antiseptic like a hospital? We recommend having hot apple cider with a cinnamon stick in one of the coffee pots – it smells like fresh apple pie – and baked cookies or a crock pot with homemade soup.

The ice cream industry had a major obstacle to overcome: There is no aroma to ice cream. How did they overcome it? As you go into a shopping center or airport, you smell waffles. The ice cream industry has associated the smell of waffles with ice cream, again bringing back childhood memories.

We want to make sure the client has something to eat before viewing the homes. You don't eat with strangers; you share food with friends. No one can ever refuse freshly baked bread or chocolate chip cookies. Make sure you have water, soda, juice, etc., a variety of drinks to offer your clients.

A funny story: One time in Dallas, we walked into a model home after the meeting with a division president, and it smelled like the house was on fire. The salesperson explained that he did exactly as I told him to do at the meeting – he put a cinnamon stick in the coffee pot and turned it on. "Did you put in the apple cider," I asked him. "No, I didn't remember that part," he said. We had a good laugh. If you put a cinnamon stick in the coffee pot and turn it on, don't forget to add the apple cider!

Greeting the Client

As the client walks in, give them eye contact and a smile. A smile is an approval-seeking behavior. We have adopted most of our behavior patterns by the time we are two to four years old. When you were that age and did something wrong, what did you do? You smiled at mom or dad. If they smiled back, you knew you weren't in trouble.

In North American culture, when we meet someone for the very first time, we smile and focus in on the eyes to see if they are looking back at us or ignoring us.

Also in North American culture, we shake hands; it is a tradition in our society. All three actions should happen at the same time: Smile, look the person in the eye, shake hands, and introduce yourself properly. What you are saying nonverbally is: "You are the most important person in the entire world to me at this very moment." There is no greater compliment you can give someone than your undivided attention.

SELLING TO FOREIGN PURCHASERS:

We revise greetings for clients from other cultures

The local market has been saturated with direct marketing for years. Every time an out of area developer enters into the market, they expect local sales; therefore, they spend their advertising dollars in the first year in the local arena with dismal results.

Colorado is South America's safe haven. The crime in their country is so rampant; initially the South Americans moved their families to the Miami area to be safe. Then in 1992, the South Americans in Dade County started migrating to Broward and Palm Beach Counties because of the rise in crime in Miami. The reason, the influx of people from South America. South Florida has increased its crime figures so much that Orlando has been considered a safe haven.

However the residents of South Florida from South America know the kidnappings there occur daily. The business owners are targets not only of the criminal, but the government as well. The mail is opened and tracked. If you mail brochures from the United States, the intended client will refuse it, fearful the government will know he is wealthy enough to have money to purchase property in the United States.

You will probably see 70% of the sales from South America with 30% coming from Brazil and 30% from Columbia. We can capture some of those clients by working the Dade and Broward markets.

First on the agenda is to sign up 'foreign international brokers' to assist us in representing you. Foreign brokers may have additional travel expenses therefore they expect a higher commission.

You'll find in the international arena, price is not a factor provided it's in the ball park. In selling to South Americans, personal relations, affiliations and bonding is critical.

In the U.S., we pride ourselves on individual independence. The South American looks for relationships and networking, in which relatives and business contacts are very important.

They are very diplomatic, have a variable sense of time, and are socially very formal. They like titles and last names and like to embrace and shake hands frequently. There is also male dominance in most parts of South America.

There are two ways to reach the foreign market.

1. Personal contacts. I can help you identify brokers and individuals who
     would most likely represent you in their respective countries.

2. Through newspaper and magazine media we can reach other potential   brokers who will find clients for us.

The South American is looking to transfer their money to the United States.
They don't care if their purchase of real estate appreciates or not. They just want to put their money in a country with a stable government. They are looking for low monthly upkeep costs on their investment.

Generally, they have no problem with a 30% down payment.

Most South Americans would like to keep their real estate as a rental unit, therefore, if you could guarantee them a tenant it will assist in a rapid sellout of the developer's property. They would use the facilities for a 30 day time period sometime during April to August.

SUGGESTED ACTION PLAN:

You will need brochures, price sheets and videos in Spanish and Portuguese, referencing square meters and square feet.

We need to capitalize on security and service.

Join the International, Columbia and Brazilian Chamber of Commerce.

We need to understand the formation of offshore corporations to insulate your client from exposure to various United States taxes. Impact of the United States estate tax can be punitive when a foreigner dies owning real estate in the United States.

Shares of a foreign corporation are not subject to United States estate taxes when held by a nonresident at the time of his death. The estate tax can be entirely avoided if the condo is owned by the foreign corporation rather that directly in the name of the foreigner.

Other advantages are avoidance of probate proceedings, avoidance of U.S. Gift tax and increased confidentiality; only the name of the offshore company and not the name of the ultimate beneficial owners of the company are filed in the public records.

COMPENSATION:

We will propose an exact budget outlining commissions, expenses, marketing costs, travel, hotel, seminar expenses, etc. which you will order and pay for plus pay a monthly retainer fee of $5,000 in advance.

There is an urgency to start as soon as possible in order to capture the summer vacationers coming up from South America.

Give them your first and last name, and in most cases, you will receive an automatic response: first and last name or title and last name. Be curious. You may be surprised at how many people define themselves by their occupation. Some define their identity through their relationship with their family. Develop ways of appealing to their sense of self.

First impressions do count, and they are the longest lasting.

Initial Information Gathering

Before you take out the floor plans, go through the model or take out the MLS book to narrow down the type of home they want.

Find out what style of home they want, how many stories they prefer, the number of bedrooms and baths, etc. Do they want a 1940's style, bungalow, or cottage retirement type of house? You can be specific in your questions.

Also, ask which exposure to the sun they prefer and why. Do they want to plant a garden? What would they plant?

Show them sample floor plans first. I prefer to have an 18 x 24 inch floor plan with only the room sizes, rather than a copy of the blue print because the blue print is too confusing for most people.

I also keep onion paper and an architectural ruler on

hand to overlay the floor plans, which gets the clients involved in planning their own home.

After the initial stage, you should know the type of home they want – size, style, layout – and the most comfortable price.

Before I leave the office to show them a home, I show the client flooring samples and ask what type of flooring they are considering. Their response indicates the level of interest they really have. The serious buyers have the floor and window treatments picked out already.
It is a minor closing technique to see if they will commit to the color of the carpet or type of flooring.

I tell them that this is a Harry-Ruth Home, for instance, as though you are presenting a signature series. I start working on building value.

When we leave the office, I prefer to take them in a golf cart or my car to be in better control of the sale.

I drive them to the property first. As I'm walking the property with them, I point out where their new home would be sitting, reconfirming the exposure they want.

Then I ask their permission to take a picture of them on the property. (I always carry my cell phone camera with me). If they say yes, they have made another subconscious commitment.

I'll pick up a rock from the lot and offer it to them. If they take it, they just purchased the home.

If I have a particular model available, I then drive them to the model. If I don't have one at hand, I show them plans and what changes they can make to customize their home, if the builder permits changes.

In the car I tell them about the celebrities and others who live in the neighborhood, the tax assessor's daughter, the three attorneys, and the doctor who will be their neighbor.

We need to fine-tune our communication abilities and have a reporting process in place, documenting in detail what has transpired with each and every prospect. It is up to us to follow up with the client in detail.

ASSOCIATION WORDS

Major corporations spend millions of dollars in decade-long campaigns, broadcasting their brands to implant their product in the clients' minds using association words. These are search engine optimized (SEO) terms that are embedded in the pitch. Examples of association words are "the Quicker Picker Upper" or "the Drink of Generations."

If I'm showing a resale home, I use association words pertaining to the materials the builder used. Here are some examples:

- Owens Corning Fiberglass

- Architectural Style Shingles

- Delta Bathroom Faucets

- American Standard Toilets

- High-Efficiency Trane Air Condition/Heat Pump

- StainMaster Carpet

- Georgia-Pacific Trusses

- Pella Windows

I can tell the client the builder builds a quality home, but they probably doubt it, as it may sound self-serving to them. As they coordinate what they hear with what they are seeing, they will draw their own conclusions.

To you as a pro it was foreknown: This is a home built with respect for their family's needs, built for the long term, and requiring very little maintenance.

Most clients ask, "How do you know the home so well?" I tell my clients before I take a listing or sell a house, I picture myself buying the home or selling it to my mother or brother. I would want the best for them, and I want the best for my clients who become my new friends.

You have to be a fact gatherer if you want to fine-tune your professional abilities.

If the school district is important to them, show them the school and say something positive about the school district.

If the son plays football, talk about how good or how forlorn the football team is.

Show them the public library and maybe give them a list of language tutors.

Find out if they attend a house of worship and ask if they want to meet Rabbi Shaw, Pastor Smith, or Father Jones. I show them the local stores where they can shop, public transportation, and any other amenity I feel might be a factor in purchasing; and guess what?

It's so critical to do upfront consulting with the clients because you can focus on the right home for them. I make the decision for them in most cases because I am the housing doctor.

If you treat them as if they have already purchased the home, they will think and act as if they already have. The Law of Pygmalion applies – you will get whatever you expect.

LAW OF EXPECTATIONS: THE PYGMALION EFFECT

Pygmalion, according to Greek Mythology, sculpted a beautiful female
statue and fell instantly and passionately in love with it. Infatuated with
his statue, he would carry it from room to room with him and shower
adoration upon it as though it were an actual living breathing woman. According to the myth, Aphrodite, the Goddess of Love, paid a visit to Pygmalion and breathed life into his statue, making it come alive.

As this law applies to selling homes, if you expect the customer to buy
one of your homes, they are more likely to buy it.

I drive them through the streets and allow them to see the rear view of the house.

I do the same from two streets back. I inform them which side of the house welcomes the morning sun and which side wishes it farewell. I point out who lives where. I show them who their friends and neighbors will be.

By this time, it is like joining the fraternity; they are in love with the idea and are anxious to see their new home. They ask, "Can we see it now?"

As I walk up to the doorway of their new home and put the key in the door, I always say as I open the door, "Welcome home."

I ask them to open the door and explain to them how the door is a little hard to open because the builder uses energy-efficient products. He has chosen a door with a magnetic seal like a refrigerator door. As they open the door, I stop at the foyer and I say, "Breathtaking! This is what your friends will see when they come over to visit." It's their WOW moment.

"Nancy, you had mentioned that the kitchen is the most important room for you because you like to cook and entertain. You said that your kitchen is small. Nancy, in this kitchen, with the large pass-through countertop, you will be able to show off your culinary talents while still entertaining your guests."

At that point, I take out a kitchen drawer and hand it to them while I talk about the quality of the drawer. I get them involved in the selling process.

I open the pantry closet and ask, "What do you keep on the floor of your pantry at home?" You will notice their eyes going to the floor of my pantry as they think about their pantry at home covered with soda bottles, potatoes, and onions. What have you just done? You have allowed them to see their belongings in their new home.
Remember the **I x V = R** formula mentioned earlier? You are using it to your advantage.

By the time you finish getting them involved in every room – placing furniture, decorating, and measuring – you have subconsciously transformed the house they were looking at into a home by creating a new self-image of them living there with their possessions.

I reduce the pressure: "If you were to consider...." Then I make a comment about their son's room. "If you were to consider living here, which room will be Joey's room?"

The master bath should have an ice bucket with a bottle of wine, wine glasses, and candles; the tub should be filled with water, and the water should have dye in it to show the flow of the water jets, if applicable, with soft music in the background. Set the stage. When you show them the master bath, don't say, "This is the master bath; it has a whirlpool tub." Instead say, "Picture yourself soaking in a bubble bath after a hard day of work, with a glass of wine and soft music in a tub built for two!" Paint the picture.

"Which wall would the bed go on? "Do you have night tables?" you would ask them. "What style and color are they? What else would you put in the bedroom? Where would you put the TV? How large is it?"

Another thing to ask is whether they plan to bring their existing furniture from their old home or buy new furniture.

Keep them involved. Keep a tape measure with you for them to measure the area where their furniture would go.

The more time you spend interacting with them, the higher the probability of your closing the sale.

The trial close that I am teaching works 90% of the time!

After I show them the home and get them involved in it, I sit in the kitchen and ask, "Before you leave, would you like me to write down some facts and figures to take home?" This approach is non-threatening, and the metamessage you are giving the client is that you don't want to waste their time and are not pressuring them to buy the home. If they have any interest in your property whatsoever – which they most likely do – they will sit down for the facts and figures. Give them documentation to take home.

Why the kitchen? It's because this is where most families gather for their serious discussions. In the kitchen I like having a round glass table and six chairs, with one of the chairs being an arm chair. The head of the family will normally sit in the armchair.

I highly recommend having a clear glass cookie jar on the table with double stuff Oreo cookies in it. For some reason, people cannot resist. You may want to have some fruit, as well, for healthy snacks.

During the summer there should be ice cream bars in the freezer for the children. Have the children go outside to eat them. The refrigerator of the model home should not have any of your personal items such as lunches in it. It should have only bottles of water or fruit juices to offer your client).

Make sure one of the bedrooms has a children's play area with DVDs to keep the children occupied while the parents are in discussion.

I sit down with them, involve them with the numbers, and show them how they cannot afford *not* to buy the home.

I draw a picture of a home on the same page as the figures with smoke coming out of the chimney to evoke a subconscious image of a warm, cozy, loving home.

I draw a dollar sign ($) inside the picture and tell them they need to be living inside their investment.

If they are in agreement with figures, I ask if I could set up an appointment with a mortgage company to take their application. Depending on which state the builder is located in, ask if I can help them fill out the mortgage application, as well, and fax it to the bank or mortgage company I've been assigned to work with.

Not everyone is easy to close. However, when a professional baseball player gets up to bat, even a top hitter will only hit the ball 30% of the time. The serious buyers who need housing will gladly sit down with you for an interview.

If you are planning to earn $100 an hour in this industry, you cannot afford to leave your office without knowing whether the client is qualified, ready, willing, and able to buy today.

Most salespeople say, "If the customer comes back two or three times, they are a real buyer." Then the salesperson is not controlling the sale!

If you are a truly professional salesperson, you only need four to six hours in front of the customer to get a contract.

As salespeople, we must use methods more sophisticated than those based on the sink-or-swim philosophies of our competitors. We need to strengthen our skills in perceiving and reacting to our clients.

In pre-selling a community, we build communities, whereas the competition builds subdivisions. I sell the lot first, since particular lots meet the client's desired exposure or size.

RELATIONSHIP SELLING
A Participation Sport

We need to get the clients involved in order to create in their minds a vivid image of them living in our home, to help the clients imagine their comfortable furniture in their new home. We build houses; the clients buy a warm, friendly home.

The competition will not be able to give them the same emotional feeling if we properly obtain at least *fifteen* subliminal subconscious commitments as we bring them through their new home.

Post-decision dissonance (buyer's remorse) will no longer be a problem if you are able to get speculations from the client as to where the furniture will go or which child will have which bedroom.

Psychologists report that if we can obtain at least fifteen subconscious descriptions, the client will consciously make a commitment to purchase the home and do whatever is necessary to follow through.

Commitment and weakness are incompatible words.

If you can't get the client to a contract, the next best thing is to get a firm date and time commitment for them to return.

If you can't get a commitment to return, ask them if they would like to invite their friends and relatives for a wine and cheese party (paid for by the builder) at the house they are thinking about purchasing. Alternately, this could be an ice cream social, a barbecue, or whatever the customer prefers. Even if the house is under construction, you can still have the party on the property they are thinking about purchasing. Since they've invited their friends and family, they have already purchased the home in their minds. The friends and family are there to validate how smart they are in purchasing the home.

During this party, the salesperson does not try to sell anybody anything. They just act as bartender or food server. The future homeowners are the stars of the show. They will proudly take their group through the home. At some point during the party, typically, a few people will walk up to the salesperson and ask, "How much is this home?" That person is probably a co-worker with the same salary range or could be a family member. They will be asking you questions about the home and how they can purchase one. Having them come to you gets you closer to the sale 99% of the time.

You can also have a housewarming party for people who have already purchased, either in their home or in the model.

Within a day after the client leaves the property, it is important to send a handwritten thank-you card.

Most builders' thank-you cards are preprinted and read: "Thanks for coming out; it's beautiful here. If you have any questions, call me." This leaves it up to the customer to follow up. Who is controlling the sale?

If you want to see magical things happen, try: "I know your time is important to you so I'll be brief (which gives them a compliment)." The second line should be something personal: "I enjoyed talking to you about your new car, boat, photography, etc." The third line should say: "I will call you Wednesday night at 7 p.m." (Give a definite day and time.)

The client now needs to consciously think about your call and discuss it with their mate and maybe with their older children. "What do you want to tell Lou when he calls?"

What greater compliment can you receive than to have them discuss buying your home without you being there? And furthermore, they are even expecting your call. In my experience, if they are not going to be home on Wednesday at 7:00, they will call you to reschedule, because you have shown them respect in the thank-you card. This is the Law of Obligation and Reciprocation.

In Relationship Selling you made a friend of a stranger. Why do you think some business is conducted on a golf or tennis court? It's hard to tell your friend that you're not purchasing from them.

MANAGEMENT

■ SALES MANAGEMENT

How To Make 'Relationship Selling' Work For You

A few pioneers are revamping every aspect of their sales processes. Trap fences are falling. Garage sales offices look more like family rooms. But this is no *soft* sell...

Kaufman and Broad's California Skylines sales office in Pittsburg, Calif., is in the garage—but the fireplace really works, the topo table is at cocktail height, and quality trimwork is everywhere. The goal is to slow prospects down and allow agents time to establish a "relationship" before showing models.

Most builders act as their own sales managers, but don't analyze sales processes as well as construction operations. Many are missing—or misinterpreting—the revolution marching under the buzzword "relationship selling."

New home sales agents are severely tested in today's marketplace, where selling cycles that once took weeks now stretch to many months. Some of the country's most analytical builders are re-engineering their sales operations—both the physical plant and their management methods—to this reality.

Florida sales consultant Lou Principe disparages model traps: "Nothing but crowd control. We're treating people like sheep when they want to be treated as individuals." Traps are vestiges of 1970s "slam-dunk" selling, where the goal was to contract buyers on the initial visit, says Principe.

He wants customers to walk in the model's front door, where agents show them into the family room or kitchen, as if they were visitors to their own home.

"The sales agent should assume the role of real estate doctor," says Principe. "The customer has a housing problem. Find out what it is."

This "bonding" is the essence of relationship selling. The sales agent assumes the role of advisor to the buyer. It takes finely honed selling skills to pull it off. But it also requires the right physical setting. One that slows visitors down, relaxes them—creates opportunity for sales agents to engage in conversation.

"Every customer walking in the door is a buyer," says Principe. "Our industry's conversion rates [sales to traffic] average 1% to 2%. A relationship selling pro will do a lot better than that."

Conventional wisdom always dictated a garage sales office with a standing-height topo table showing lots available—and sold. But that environment doesn't fit relationship selling.

Shown here is one builder's turn on the new breed. The sales office at

Law of Expectations and the Pygmalion Effect

Builders and brokers need to realize that they have a Pygmalion effect on the sales team. Whatever you expect, you will get, and therefore, I am asking you set the bar higher.

IMPROVED SELF-IMAGE

When your salespeople first got hired, they were excited to come into your company for the interview. The night before, they laid out their best clothing, shoes, and accessories. They could hardly sleep that night they were so excited. Then they get hired. Their dream comes true. This is called the "honeymoon stage." Happiness abounds as in the honeymoon stage of a marriage.

The new team members are anxious to be well liked by the rest of the team. Instead, they are told to make coffee and run errands. While they are running errands, they are not on the floor taking customers. This is why they are typically told they will not sell anything for 90 days. The existing salespeople don't want the competition. At this point, the new salespeople go into what is called the "accommodation" stage.

If they lose their excitement during this stage, they go into the "toleration" stage where they have become disillusioned and unhappy. Many of them quit or become uninspired and mediocre salespeople.

Typically, 20% of your sales team is comprised of top achievers, 20% are bottom achievers, and 60% are mediocre. That 60% will rise to the top with a motivational type seminar such as the one I teach.

Leaders need to create a new self-image for their entire team. It is imperative to help your team refresh their skills and reinvigorate their excitement for sales. As a leader, you must help your team rediscover why they do what they do and create a sense of urgency in doing it.

The salespeople need to be trained *before* they get into the sales office and then they should be allowed to start selling immediately. Most developers tell people that they won't make any money for 90 days when in fact, I have shown countless salespeople how to make one sale per week. Most sales trainers tell the salespeople what to do but have never done it themselves. But once the new salespeople employ the new approach, they become illuminated and ascend to a level of professionalism that only a small handful of real estate people working for builders throughout the United States have achieved.

Some builders impede the results of the salespeople by having limited hours of availability. For instance, throughout the United States from 9:00 am -12:00 pm Monday morning most national builders demand their people be in a meeting. But perhaps the customer came out Saturday afternoon to look at the home and came back Sunday afternoon with their family (assuming you were open on Sunday).

They talked about it Sunday night and decided to buy the home first thing Monday. But your model homes are closed on Monday morning because everyone is in the main office having a sales meeting!

You would do well to expand your hours of availability to your clients, including expanding evening hours to accommodate various schedules.

Go to any security gate in a luxury subdivision after 7:00 pm and ask the security guard how many people come in between 7:00 to 11:00 pm asking if the models are open. The guard normally responds that there are a few of these people every night. I then ask the guard if the prospective buyers are in late model expensive cars. They usually answer in the affirmative – yes. These are professional physicians, attorneys, and business people who work 24/7 and can only come out to look at a luxury home after hours, but your hours don't accommodate them. Why? Customers must always come first!

At one high end condominium complex in Miami Beach, the sales manager went home at his normal time, 5:30 pm, just as a customer was coming in the door. He asked me to take care of the customer. By the time I finished with the customer the next day, I had sold him a $1.5 million penthouse earning a $50,000 plus commission. Had he extended his office hours, he may have made the sale himself.

Safe Uncle Theory

Doctor Glasser, a noted psychologist, explains the "Safe Uncle" theory:

"If you the manager tell your employees they are doing something incorrectly, and they admit to it, they are also admitting the manager is smarter than they are, which can result in bruised egos. Performance levels stay the same. However, when an outside consultant, a safe "Uncle Louie" says basically the same thing, there is no contest because he not a direct threat.

CEO of US Home Bob Strudler introduced me to senior management in the following way: "Lou's an outside consultant with an objective set of eyes."

I worked free for three weeks in the Tampa Division of US Home. Dean Bill Manck of the Small Business Development Center from USF attended my classes at US Home Tampa and published an article in the Small Business Development Journal):

"Within a 21 day period, closing rates went from 2% to 25%, a 1,000%, Increase:

Small
Business
Development
Center

Colleg
Univer
Tampa

PRINCIPE'S PRINCIPLE

Louis C. Principe offers increased sales within a one-month period, or your money back! Sounds impossible, right? WRONG. This man is serious.

A St. Petersburg-based real estate sales consultant, Principe prefers to be called a "psychological educator." The fact that he has never had to return any money is tribute to his ability to make good on his offer. Principe specializes in teaching communications skills which can aid in generating sales. Yet even in the face of his success Principe asserts, "No one can motivate anyone else. I can only teach others how to do it themselves."

After 18 years of real estate sales experience, this self-educated student of psychology combined the disciplines. In addition, he set out to change management's attitude toward employees. "What affect does management have on employees?" asks Principe, "and what affect does the individual have on himself?" He believes that upgrading an individual's self esteem can lead to a dramatic increase in productivity. "Most people aren't successful," says Principe, "because they don't think they can be successful."

One of his case histories is from a local builder of higher quality homes. The company was experiencing a 2% closing rate. After their sales representatives completed Principe's program, the rate jumped to 25%. This constituted a 1000% increase in productivity. Similar success stories are evident in a notebook filled with testimonial letters praising Principe's effective approach.

So valuable was the program I taught that I was sought after competitively by many major builders to teach these seminars.

I'd like to teach you the same techniques I taught them, so you, too, can become a real estate consultant for builders and realtors.

PHILOSOPHY

The Principe Program is interactive. It includes a wide range of activities from discussions and exercises to role-playing and simulations. We want the attendees to experience each new technique in a way that it becomes internalized. *Tell me and I'll forget; show me and I may remember; involve me and I'll understand.*

We know that individual learning occurs through mental associations rather than through memorization. That someone can memorize and regurgitate does not indicate that they have acquired advanced knowledge.

Individual learning occurs through experience based on circumstances, environment, and association with others. Learning occurs most effectively when the individual is challenged in a supportive environment. People only learn what they want to learn.

The Principe Method

Our method involves unlearning lifelong habits and assumptions and forsaking deeply held beliefs about how to sell real estate. Motivation and inspiration must be woven into the learning module in order for the person to internalize it.

We have received hundreds of letters from thousands of people who have attended this program. Documented evidence supports the singular novelty of this program and the outstanding result attendees achieve.

Our mission is to educate people in the highest form of intelligence – social intelligence – the ability to communicate effectively and efficiently with people using the soft skills, which are the hardest to learn because of the subconscious manner in which they occur.

There are no line items in your profit and loss statement for what we measure, which is what is in the hearts and minds of your sales team. That is where your profitability lies. Your front line employee, the person who answers the phone, the delivery driver—everyone who comes into contact with the public—should be thoroughly trained on how to sell your product.

Your team members need to realize that the customer who walks in the door or calls on the phone potentially wants to buy your product. That inquiry may turn into a sale, but only if the sales person treats the customer as a buyer and not just as an annoying caller who wanted information.

These psychological skills will not only benefit the professional sales of real estate agents and developers, but will also help them in their personal lives, as well. It is well known that family life affects success at work.

You have the ability to make another person's mind receptive to what you are saying and the means to steer clients, your listeners, to respond affirmatively. Not "no," not "maybe", but **"Yes.". "Si." "是!"**

We have it within us, but we all need to fine-tune ourselves introspectively. This is like a tuning an old television set; move the knob just a hair and the reception comes in perfectly.

We are creatures of conditioned reflex. Once a response pattern is established in terms of persuasion, then we can persuade people to do almost anything.
You will need to think outside the box, to accept challenges, and to stretch your sometimes stubborn minds.

Developing superior human communication will do more for a person's self-image than anything else, according to psychologist Sydney Jourard.
Most of the problems in life stem from the inability to get along with others. This is the primary reason for frustration, failure, broken families, unemployment, termination from employment, excessive use of alcohol and drugs, negative attitudes, depression, and fatigue.

STOP THE EXCUSES

Let's look for reasons to excel beyond our expectations.

Aristotle taught centuries ago that people are creatures of habit. It is natural to avoid new thoughts because they upset our habits. Someone has moved the furniture; it's a new experience. A foreign language is foreign until you learn it.

Aristotle taught that if you don't learn something as a youth and someone approaches you later in life about a new idea, your first reaction is to reject it because you don't want to consciously think about it.
Western Union turned down Alexander Graham Bell, because they thought it foolish to talk over wires.

We need to become visionaries. Dr. Albert Einstein said that creativity and imagination are more important than education because "with creativity and imagination I can show people things they cannot see."

In my seminars I show people things they didn't know existed inside themselves – things that will bring them a more rewarding life.

I teach Aristotle's techniques of persuasive speech and how to measure it, as well as the barriers to it. In addition, I show people how to recognize a personality type. I show my students more effective learning and listening styles. I also teach Einstein's philosophy concerning goal setting, communication, and success.

Set your goals higher. A dream is only a dream until you write it down. Have a picture of it in your mind; it goes from "thin air" to a palpable plan, a blueprint, the groundwork, and eventually a commitment to making the plan materialize. At that point, it becomes an achievable goal. Commitment and weakness are not compatible conditions.

"Excellence is an art won by training and habituation. We are what we repeatedly do. Excellence, then, is not an act, but a habit." – Aristotle

"You can lead a horse to water, but you can't make it drink. However you can salt the oats to make it thirsty." Lou Principe

OUTLINE FOR 'HOW TO PRE-SELL A HOME' SEMINAR

Objective of seminars:

To get commitment, i.e., business trip reservation, appointment to see agent in their home, or telephone appointment.

I.   **ACTUAL PRINT CAMPAIGN**

II.   **AERIAL PHOTOS**

III.   **PHYSICAL ARRANGEMENTS**

A. Tables & Chairs - Herringbone Fashion

B. Displays around room

C. Map, blow up of warranty program & flip charts for each table.

IV. **ACKNOWLEDGEMENT OF SPONSORS:** MC: I'd like to acknowledge our sponsors for this public service seminar: SunTrust Bank, Prudential Florida Realty and Avatar Holdings.

V. **INTRODUCTION OF SPEAKER LOU PRINCIPE**

MC: "I would like to introduce Lou Principe who has lived throughout Florida for over fifty years and recently moved to Pueblo, Colorado. He has lectured at several universities throughout the United States and founded both the Principe Institute of Real Estate and The Florida Real Estate College, which present ongoing educational courses.

Lou is here today not only as a consumer advocate but also as friend, teacher and lecturer. He has authored a booklet entitled "Colorado Retirement Real Estate Guide." Everyone in attendance will receive a free copy at the end of this seminar.

And now, Lou Principe...."

VI. **LOU BEGINS PRESENTATION**

A. LP: "I'll ask some questions before we start. Depending on the answers, I'll know how to customize this seminar to each individual's personality, learning and listening styles.

- "Do you, own, rent, vacation. or live here, retired from....

- "Who is planning to relocate out of area?

- "Do those of you planning to relocate have a home to sell?

- "If so, do you plan to sell this year or next?

- "Who has started to look already?"

- (I'll talk about location and economic growth.)

- "Are you planning on purchasing a second home? Interested in mountains, healthy air and thriving economy?"

B. I discuss types of property found in Colorado: Single family, condo, and manufactured.

C. I discuss how location & economic outlook determine growth factor and risk envelope.

D. I'll mention the growth in Colorado and what it's going to be like in 10 years.

VI. POWER POINT PRESENTATION (LOU)

"When people move, they look for these things:

- Lower cost of living

- Improved health

57

- New friends and activities

- More choices for housing

"You need to judge your next community by:

- Climate and environment

- Health facilities and amenities – hospitals, clinics, doctors, and specialists

- Housing costs and availability

- Cost of living

- Proximity to houses of worship

- Leisure time activities (Colorado has tons)

- Scenery and views – striking landscaping such as trees and shrubs

- Pollution

- Noise

- Shopping

- Services: banks, postal, legal, etc.

- Police and fire protection

- Transportation

- Surrounding areas

- Health advantages (access to bike or hiking trails, etc.)

- Quality of water

- Nursing homes and home care facilities

- Taxes

- Job availability

- Energy costs

- Reasonably priced services: plumbing, handymen, carpentry, and repair of all kinds

"Health officials claim you live longer in Colorado than in any other state because of climate and because deaths from principal diseases of old age decline – heart disease and diabetes – are well below the national average.

Cost of living is generally lower in Colorado."

VII.   THE CLOSE (LOU)

"I've consulted for dozens of developers throughout the United States. I've lived in Florida, New York, New Jersey, Michigan, California, Alabama, and Mississippi, and spent at least a month with builders in every major city in the US. When it was time for me to retire, I came to the conclusion that there is no better retirement area than Pueblo/Trinidad, Colorado as far as health, real estate prices, beautiful seasons, air quality, low crime rate compared to other cities, wonderful friendly people, fresh organic food, and a strong traditional spiritual richness that I have not found in any other city."

A. Discuss the history and highlights of the cities.

B. Show Power Point of various selling points of the area, including economy, population and land mass.

C. Compare traffic and crime stats.

D. Give example of highlights for the city:

- Southern Colorado will have more than _____ people living there. And _____ people per square mile on 138,000 plotted lots.

- The population today is _____ year-round residences. It has _____ single family detached lots with an average size of _____.

- You can live like a king in an $85,000 home; that's why it's called The New Wave Community.

- Southern Colorado is ___% below the cost of living index for the nation. By comparison, New York was 232% above, San Diego was 122.8% above, and Atlanta was 100.9%.

- Schools: The pupil-teacher ratio is _____. There are __ elementary schools, ___ middle schools, ___ high schools, and ___ colleges or universities, with over ___ of the schools being awarded the "Blue Ribbon of Excellence."

E. Colorado is everything for everybody, "a multigenerational/cultural kingdom."

- Fishing paradise

- Outdoor sports: golf, tennis, cycling, boating, sailing, hiking, climbing, horseback riding, and skiing

- Cultural areas

- Schools

- Music venues

- Houses of Worship

- Unusually attractive homes

- Low cost of hospital facilities

AARP SENIOR HOUSING SURVEY

- 28% live alone. Only 5% live in a retirement community

Wants:

- 30% Common interests

- 24% Quiet/peaceful ambiance

- 20% Social activities

- 18% Helpful friends and neighbors

- 17% Friendly people

- 59% Pharmacy

- 54% Doctor's office

- 49% Hospital

- 65% Walking distance to a grocery store.

- 17% Have moved within the past 5 years.

- 26% Moved to a different city or county in the same state.

- 76% Prefer to live in a neighborhood with people of all ages.

- 34% Prefer living in a small town.

- 25% Pprefer the country.

- 25% Prefer suburbs.

- 13% Prefer a city.

- All subgroups prefer small towns.

Of lesser importance:

- 39% Public transportation

- 35% Proximity to children or grandchildren

- 35% Cultural resources

- 26% Senior center

- 21% Recreational facilities

- 64% Concerned about utilities

- 61% Concerned about property taxes

- 59% Maintenance costs

- 58% Concerned with crime

- Age group most wanting to move: 55 - 64

- 21% Divorced, separated, or never married

- 22% Renters

- Of people who moved within the past 5 years, 35% of those 55 and older say they have done no planning at all for their future housing needs, and 18% have done only a little.

- 22% Expect to move

- 13% Would really like to move

- Only 12% consulted with someone about where to live.

"Colorado is the "New Wave Community" that is referred to in Understanding Senior Housing, a study done by the AARP. A New Wave Community is nationally designed exclusively as intergenerational to provide diverse opportunities for each person 'to be all he or she can be.'"

"Boomers in their late 40s and early 50s are the most affluent group, and are the biggest spenders. Boomers need to be reminded that adventure awaits.

"Let's talk about the developer. Who is the developer?

"If, after hearing this, you have reached the conclusion that thousands of others have already reached about Colorado, I am recommending you to take a business trip with me. "How many would like to have a fun weekend in Colorado?" [Asks for show of hands. NOTE: If the presenter raises their hand, they will receive an automatic response of the majority of people raising their hand.]

"If any of you wish to go with me, for only [insert dollar amount] per couple or single, you get transportation, hotel for three nights, and a free tour." (This is for people who wish to fly from out of state to view the Colorado property. Some may wish to purchase sight unseen).

"HOME BUYING SEMINARS ARE THE LEAST EXPENSIVE ADVERTISING THAT GETS SALES."

F. QUESTIONS AND ANSWERS

PRINCIPE'S PRINCIPLES FOR PROFESSIONALS

- Achieving goals
- Apperception: The Greatest Principle of Selling
- Automatic Behavior Patterns and Subconscious Reactions
- Communication: Voice, Tone & Non-verbal signals
- Deficiencies in Listening: The major source of wasted time, miscarried plans, and frustrated decisions
- Five Steps to Change
- Gorilla Marketing: Unique tools for Develops, Builders & Realtors
- How to get 'yes' answers
- How to list subdivisions from builders, developers, and banks
- International Buyers
- Laws of Society
- Leadership Delegation: Gopher vs. Stewardship
- Leadership Skills
- Listening skills: How to hear the underlying message
- Motivation: A greater impact on learning than any other cognitive aspects of the learner's situation
- Marketing Yourself: People Buy People
- Organizational skills

- Overcoming objections
- Post-dissonance (buyer's remorse)
- Problem solving skills: What steps to take in any situation
- Proper use of the telephone: why the phone is critical
- Pygmalion Management: Law of Expectations
- Reticular formations: How to gain one's attention

- To maximize performance: Instilling a greater sense of teamwork, company pride, and personal commitment among program participants (can be shared with co-workers, family members, and society.)
- Time management: Do you confuse activity with accomplishment?
- Transformational Learning: Holds the greatest potential for human growth.

About the Author:

Lou Principe ("Uncle Lou") went from a front line salesperson for builders to an international sales trainer and speaker. He has been presenting real estate seminars, motivational speeches, and customer service trainings for over fifty years. Lou has trained many Fortune 100 companies including the top national home builders and such organizations as ATT, Bell South, Merrill Lynch Private Fund, University of Central Florida, and University of North Florida, just to name a few.

Lou served as an adjunct professor at University of North Florida, and as a Senior Associate of University of Central Florida. He founded the Florida Real Estate College and the Principe Institute, which partnered with both universities to promote his real estate and motivational seminars.

Lou's passion for helping the homeless, the unemployed, the underemployed, and the prison population has propelled him to design a successful program to integrate these individuals into society. Lou has found creative and unique ways to merge his passion for real estate and helping these groups.

Lou is a published author of numerous books and articles which can all be found on his three websites.

Lou currently lives in Pueblo, Colorado, where he spends most of his time enjoying the four perfect mild seasons, reading, golfing, walking, exploring and promoting Southern Colorado, by teaching others to become more successful in their lives.

You may find more information on my seminars and trainings, along with contact information, on the websites below:
www.SellYourWayToSuccess.com

Sincerely,
Lou Principe, The Real Estate Doctor